Almost T0149938

Peter Valente is a translator for whom every poet should hope. A distinguished poet, Valente possesses an exceptionally fine sense of the English language. Fluent in Italian and French as well, he renders the celebrated multilingual Swiss poet Pierre Lepori in nuanced English. Valente's is an achievement of a remarkably high order, a great translation of a major book.

—**Edward Foster**, author of *A Looking-Glass for Traytors*

Almost Love bristles with imagery that is both startling and timeless, drawing us onto a love-road that branches towards eternity. In this epic work, Swiss poet Pierre Lepori effortlessly pulls the reader into a Jacob's ladder of passion and despair. Separately, each stanza is a small jewel—linked together, they are truly dazzling. Beautifully translated by the poet Peter Valente, *Almost Love* is a work that shines brightly in these dark times.

—**Maggie Dubris**, author of *Skels: A Novel*

In Pierre Lepori's *Almost Love*, the language is so disciplined, thus ravishing, the reader is able to transcend grief as undertone and focus instead on "the threshold of life" where tentativeness can be a small light towards an opening. Certainty can be a "stupid column" and this poetry surfaces from the ecstasy of a language attuned to how the lover's image is what is reflected on "a beam of light / the breath kept / in the hollow of the hand" as it writes.

—**Eileen R. Tabios**, author of *Dovelion: A Fairy Tale for our Times*

In these highly metaphoric and charged love poems the beloved becomes not just the characteristic object of desire, but the embodiment of desire itself. "There are doors open everywhere," writes Lepori. Peter Valente has found each door the poet has opened and marvelously manages to convey for English readers the resonance, depth, beauty and language of Lepori's originals.

—**Christopher Sawyer-Lauçanno**, translator and author of *Remission*

Through a consanguinity of sculptural space and tormented silences, Peter Valente's exquisite *Almost Love* erupts as a mereology, a mirrorology of aching hunger in the ferocity of desire. Riddled with arced echoes, madness and rigor; suspension, fragilities, agilities; pulsing partitas of lettered skin threshold in an erotics of meaning and being caressing and elevating the other and the other in language. With magnificent intensity, between dawns, bodies, fingers hauntings, lairs; between the "as if" and the "always already," *Almost Love* will leave you forever absorbed in the textatically shadowed constructions of trembling eros.

—**Adeena Karasick**, *Salomé: Woman of Valor*

With its passionate echoes of Sappho and Cavafy, and the querulous shadow of Barthes, Lepori's *Almost Love* continues the ageless attempt to fix the beloved in an ever-shifting sky. Anguish and ardor fuse in an idiom of invocation and idolatry, with an intimation of torn papyrus, or rolled parchment in a marble box. Yet Peter Valente's sleek translation reveals the freshness of these timeless tropes, their inescapable resonance with our own personal mysteries. The leanness and immediacy of the language turns sentimentality into wonder, and the pure contrary intellect of Eros burns free.

—**Aaron Shurin**, author of *The Blue Absolute*

The absence of a lover's response in Pierre Lepori's *Almost Love* is as powerful as the absence of light. The poet is consumed with his love and the lover—"my love has lands bathed in rain / and white suns in the fold of the knee." His love is tangible, intangible, sexual, mythic, and like the wind. When the poet begins to separate from his love, first a period of analysis, then as the veil lifts, barrenness and bitterness. As with Orpheus, if one tries too hard, love evaporates. The "we" flounders without a verb, but then Lepori moves from the wild longing that obscures sight and vision into a quiet acceptance of the shortness of love, of life. With the end of the love affair, whether imaginary or real, the love and the lover remain beautifully inscribed in Lepori's poems.

—**Barbara Henning**, author of *Digigram*

In this bracing sequence of quasi-amorous poems, Pierre Lepori subjects both his emotions and the language in which he expresses them to clinical self-scrutiny. He is especially skilled at reading the precise calibrations of proximity and distance involved in loving and in speaking of love. Each entangled in tight knots of feeling, two lovers confront and turn away from each other, as the development of their relationship demands. In Peter Valente's incisive translations, the language of love is spare and clear, as transparent as a finely-ground lens.

　　　　—**Gregory Woods,** author of *Records of an Incitement to Silence*

It's almost impossible to translate a poem. A translation is like a reflection of a lover in a mirror you cannot kiss although you see his lips. What's remarkable about Peter Valente's translation of *Almost Love* is that there is a kiss; there is nothing almost about it. Pierre Lepori's Italian is beautiful, but so is Peter Valente's English. I've read *Almost Love* several times now and love the poems because they're real, the experience, not its reminiscence; when they tell you they love you, you hear them loud and clear. I can't imagine anyone not sensually enjoying them.

　　　　—**Don Yorty,** author of *Spring Sonnets*

Almost Love

GUERNICA WORLD EDITIONS 48

With the support
of the TT3 Association (Lausanne)

Almost Love

PIERRE LEPORI

Translated by Peter Valente

An Italian-English Bilingual Edition

TORONTO—CHICAGO—BUFFALO—LANCASTER (U.K.)

2022

Guernica Founder: Antonio D'Alfonso

Michael Mirolla, editor
Interior design: Jill Ronsley, suneditwrite.com
Cover design: Allen Jomoc Jr.

Guernica Editions Inc.
287 Templemead Drive, Hamilton (ON), Canada L8W 2W4
2250 Military Road, Tonawanda, N.Y. 14150-6000 U.S.A.
www.guernicaeditions.com

Distributors:
Independent Publishers Group (IPG)
600 North Pulaski Road, Chicago IL 60624
University of Toronto Press Distribution (UTP)
5201 Dufferin Street, Toronto (ON), Canada M3H 5T8
Gazelle Book Services, White Cross Mills
High Town, Lancaster LA1 4XS U.K.

First edition.
Printed in Canada.

Legal Deposit—First Quarter
Library of Congress Catalog Card Number: 2021951194
Library and Archives Canada Cataloguing in Publication
Title: Almost Love / Pierre Lepori ; translated by Peter Valente.
Names: Lepori, Pierre, 1968- author. | Valente, Peter, 1970- translator. | container
of (work): Lepori, Pierre, 1968- Quasi amore. | container of (expression): Lepori,
Pierre, 1968- Quasi amore. English.
Series: Guernica world editions ; 48.
Description: Italian-English bilingual edition. | Series statement: Guernica world
editions ; 48 | Poems. | Translation of: Quasi amore. | Poems in Italian and English;
translated from the Italian.
Identifiers: Canadiana 2021037991X | ISBN 9781771837354 (softcover)
Classification: LCC PQ5961.9.L47 A713 2022 | DDC 851/.92—dc23

These brief moments are like the leaves that grow
like the flowers of youth,
unaware of what the gods have in store
whether good or bad.
   —Mimnermus

I

il mio amore è dappertutto
è vento talvolta tempesta
tiepido all'inizio dell'estate
rigido d'inverno

II

dall'ovale dell'oblò
le nubi appaiono per
quello che sono
vapore a banchi che galleggia
gomma piuma da sfiorare
zucchero che non seduce
ed è il mio amore così
un tappeto di batuffoli
gocce che salgono
spinte dal proprio dissiparsi
spinte dal vento
il mio amore è bianco e lento

I

my lover is everywhere
sometimes he's a storm
tepid at the beginning of summer
rigid[1] in winter

II

in the oval of the porthole
the clouds stand for
what I am
fog on seats floating
foam from dizzying heights
sugar that isn't sweet
and my love is so like
a carpet of cotton balls
droplets that rise
pushed by the wind
driven by a desire to spread
my love is pure and slow

---

[1] In the sense of being "erect."

III

dove vai amore mio?
tu che vai se mi volto
tu che vai e scompari
eppure il tuo alito sul collo
non è illusione
è la vita stretta
l'ardore
il poco di me che resta
quando ti guardo e non ti vedo
quando mi guardi e non mi vedi
amore che è un semplice nome
nella risacca delle ore

IV

il mio amore ha mani grandi
come il verso di una canzone
ma il mio amore è una canzone banale
sciocco esagerato
modulato in minore
il mio amore

il mio amore ha pace nel ventre
e nodi di pianto
braccia e gambe in un gomitolo di carni
il mio amore ha terre di pioggia
e soli bianchi nella piega del ginocchio
non brucia né ferisce
neppure quando è notte

III

my love where are you going?
you who always leave when I turn my back
you who leave and disappear
but your breath on my neck
is not a dream
this is the disciplined life
the ardor
the little of me that remains
when I look at you I do not see you
when you look at me you do not see me
my love that has a simple name
in the passage of the hours

IV

my lover has large hands
like in the song[2]
but my love-song is banal
foolish and exaggerated
my love is modulated
in a minor key

my lover is at peace in his belly
from the knot that precedes tears
the arms and legs in a tangle of flesh
my love has lands bathed in rain
and white suns in the fold of the knee
it doesn't burn or hurt
even at night

---

[2] The song is "Senza Fina" by Luigi Tenco.

V

il mio amore ha numeri negli occhi
e pensieri di troppo

VI

quando parla se parla
ha la mia stessa voce
ma in lingue diverse e molteplici
come sono diverse tutte
le lingue di una mano

non importa se siamo lontani
se ha piedi di pioggia
non importa se è a credito il suo sorriso
non importa se piango

V

my lover has numbers in his eyes
and thinks too much

VI

when he speaks if he speaks
he uses my voice
but the languages are different and numerous
just as the languages of a hand
are all so different

it doesn't matter if we are apart
or if he has feet of rain
it doesn't matter if the smile doesn't last
it doesn't matter if I cry

VII

in questa città che profuma di noi
che ti fa vivo e vegeto
il corpo prova la leggerezza dell'infanzia
forse è la lingua di qui
aspra e solenne che ci tiene a distanza

e camminiamo come mai camminammo
come un riflesso di sole nel bicchiere
posati sul ciglio di un tavolo
sulla soglia della vita

VIII

il mio amore ha occhi di sfinge
spalancati al volere della sera
nessuno li può guardare a lungo
quanto me
perché assorbono tutto
parole comprese

occhi che pendono dal soffitto
più azzurri della voce di un angelo
con perfezione assoluta
dentro di me da sempre
così come in loro io sono
assorbito

VII

in this city that smells of us
where you're doing ok
the body feels the lightness of childhood
maybe it's the harsh and solemn language here
that keeps us apart

and we walked what made us walk
like the reflection on a glass
placed on the edge of a table
we walked on the threshold of life

VIII

my lover has eyes like the sphinx
wide open according to the will of the night
no one can look at them for as long
as I can
because they absorb everything
including the words

eyes hanging from the ceiling
bluer than the voice of an angel
absolutely perfect
within me forever
just as I am absorbed
in them

IX

se m'intuassi come io t'inmio
amore
amore mio

X

vista dall'alto la nostra città
ha gioco facile a sembrarci bellissima
tepore di una sera di maggio
una sera regale

l'angelo di Mehringplatz
ha semplici e forti le ali
ormeggiate alle scapole elastiche
e lo sguardo di mina di piombo
sui giardini divelti dal vento

e noi sediamo sotto un tiglio o un ontano
sembriamo uno e non lo siamo
parliamo ad alta voce
come bambini fortunati
fragili nel gioco
che ci siamo inventati

l'amore per quello che è
poco meno della vita

IX

If I were in you as you are in me[3]
O love
my love

X

it's easy to find our city
so beautiful from above
on a warm May evening
a royal evening

this angel of the Mehringplatz[4]
has simple and strong elastic wings
tied to his shoulder blades
and his eyes are very dark
as he gazes down upon the wind-torn gardens

we sit under a lime or an alder tree
to a viewer I seem alone but my lover is present
we raise our voices
as lucky children
fragile in the game
that we invented

the love for that which is
slightly less real than life

---

[3] The line, "se m'intuassi come io t'inmio" is from the Paradiso (Book IX) of Dante's *Divine Comedy*.
[4] The Goddess of Victory, which the Berliners also call the Friedensengel (The Angel of Peace) is a statue on top of a column in the middle of the Mehringplatz in Berlin.

XI

pace dice l'angelo
sulla colonna sciocca
delle umane certezze
nella sua mano tracce di sudore
che lappo come un cane
fedele alle promesse
della tua quieta assenza
che nessun altro vede
sulla piazza in cantiere
nell'ora quarta del crepuscolo

il mio amore ha ali grandi
non ha paura di dispiegarle
solo per me

XI

be at peace says the angel
on top of the stupid column
of human certainty
in its hands traces of sweat
that I lap up like a dog
faithful to the promise
of your quiet absence
that no one notices
in the square on the construction site
at 4pm

my lover has large wings
and is not afraid to deploy them
just for me

XII

vorrei lo sai non essere
sciocco e petulante
quando l'ansia mi stinge alla gola
e temo il giorno come la salamandra ama il fuoco
e giurerei di averti visto nello specchio
appena dietro alle mie spalle
nel guizzo opaco di una piastrella del bagno
in queste stanze non mie non nostre
in questa dolce ottusa città di primavera
nell'angolo del letto che gli ingenui
chiamano attesa
e che io chiamo amore

XII

I wish I wasn't
so silly and petulant
whenever anxiety stings my throat
I fear the day as the salamander loves the fire
and I swear I saw you in the mirror
just behind me
in the opaque flicker upon the bathroom tile
in these rooms that are not mine or ours
in this sweet dull city in Spring
lying on the edge of the bed the naïve people call
this a dream of hope
but I call it love

XIII

abbi pietà luce del giorno
se il mio amore non viene al tatto
ma occorre gridare e gemere
scegliere cieli ricoperti di graffi
squame di pioggia alla finestra

mentre mi copro con la coperta il capo
perché il ronzio della tua assenza
il clangore del mio amore che tarda
non ingorghi il palato

XIV

e giorno ti prego rendi semplici le parole
giacché l'acqua che chiara conduce
al mio amore che si nasconde tra le pieghe
sia solenne e casta
limpida come l'aggettivo
ovvia come la voce nel canto
e le illusioni sempre più leggere
meno ingombre di luoghi comuni

XIII

O light of day be merciful
if my lover does not respond to my touch
but we must shout and moan
choose scratched skies
flakes of freezing rain at the window

while I cover my head with a blanket
because of the buzz of your absence
the clangor of my late love
doesn't choke me

XIV

O light of day please make the words simple
for the clear water leads
to my lover who hides himself between the folds
either solemn and chaste
clear as the obvious adjective
as the voice in the song
and the illusions increasingly lightweight
less cluttered with platitudes

XV

il mio amore viene e non viene
si apposta sul ciglio del dire
nella fragilità di queste dita
da cui il miele e la mirra

XVI

poi mi prende la notte
mi gira tra le mani e sputa lava
per coprire di neve calda il petto

il mio amore è amaro
e nell'amarlo consiste la sua voce
non conosce la distanza

XV

my lover appears and vanishes
on the edge of a word
in the brittleness of these fingers
from which
honey and myrrh …

XVI

then the night takes me
it turns me around with its hands and it spits
it washes me covering my chest with hot snow

my love is bitter
and in my love his voice resides
unaware of distance

XVII

il mio amore ne ha abbastanza
e vorrebbe rigirare il guanto
buttarmi in faccia le cuciture e le ferite
ma al mio amore volto le spalle
alzo un muro perché faccia finta di niente
e il mio amore torna docile nel grembo
sceglie di fondersi nel fragile seno
dell'avambraccio
mi abbraccia e mi consola

XVIII

solitudine è una buona definizione
del mio amore dalle ali di stoffa lacera
un treno imbocca la stazione
piegandosi di lato e cigolando
ci sono porte aperte ovunque
non le vedi al primo sguardo
ma senti un leggero movimento
dell'aria e segui il vento

XVII

my lover has had enough
and would like to turn the glove[5] around
throw the seams and the wounds of life in my face
I turn my back on my love
I put up a wall and act like I don't care
and my lover now returns docile in my lap
chooses to melt in the fragile skin of my elbow
embraces me
and consoles me

XVIII

solitude is a good way to define
my love from the torn cloth of these wings
a train enters the station
bending around the side and crawling
there are doors open everywhere
you do not see him at first glance
but you feel a slight movement in the air
and you follow the wind

---

[5] This suggests the line "a sentence is but a cheveril glove to a good wit" from Shakespeare, *The Twelfth Night* (Act III, Scene I).

XIX

il mio amore ha la bellezza del vento
quando scende sui ricordi e lucida i prati
il mio amore ha capelli d'un biondo pallido
e stivali delle sette leghe per corrermi incontro
il mio amore è ogni angolo di strada
e occhi bui di tarda notte senza pianto

XX

per capire da dove venga e dove andiamo
il mio amore mi costringe a studiare
i fondi del caffè

XIX

my love is beautiful like the wind
when it descends it polishes memories and the fields
my lover's hair is light blond
and he wears seven-league boots[6] when he meets me
my lover is on every street corner
with dark eyes late at night and without tears

XX

to understand where my lover comes from and where he goes
my love forces me to study
the coffee grinds

---

[6] The mythical pair of boots mentioned in various fairy tales, originally popularized in the tales of Charles Perrault, that allowed the wearer to travel a great length (seven leagues) with each step.

XXI

il mio amore ha piccole mani
mani piccole e piccolo dolore
che scandisce il tempo
di tanto in tanto
sotto il folto agitarsi della bocca

XXII

posso coglierlo su un viso qualunque
il mio amore che esiste e non esiste

è il riflesso di un raggio
il respiro trattenuto
nel cavo di una mano

XXI

my lover has small hands
small hands and minor pain
that marks time on occasion
under your mouth's vast agitation

XXII

my lover exists and does not exist
I receive his image from any face

in the reflection of a beam of light
the breath kept
in the hollow of the hand

XXIII

s'alza in volo la sua voce
ed è una bianca melodia
quasi un canto mattutino di cemento
nei prati seminati a neve fresca
nei treni in corsa
nello schiumare
assurdo
dei giorni

XXIV

la gioventù è un dato di fatto?

XXIII

his voice rises
and it's a pure melody
almost a morning song of cement
in the fields covered with fresh snow
in the speeding trains
seething at
the absurdity
of days

XXIV

Is youth real?

XXV

esercizi di osservazione disciplinata
l'amore in forma di rosa
sudore e pianto

XXVI

ripete inguaribile le parole
senza paura della tela bianca
dell'usura e del tempo

qui tutto è sospeso leggero
nel breve taglio di un sogno
tra il silenzio e la voce

tra ciò che esiste in un pensiero
e l'avverarsi della pelle
anche solo sulla pagina

XXV

exercises of disciplined observation
love in the form of a rose
sweat and tears

XXVI

hopelessly repeated the words
without fear of the white canvas
of the wear and tear of time

here everything is suspended and subtle
in the short cut to dream
between the silence and the voice

between what exists in a thought
and the occurrence of skin
even on the page

XXVII

la bellezza è in sé un amore
sedimentato nello sguardo
un'arenaria di ricordi
di baci di carezze di respiri
quando sul limite del cielo
a capofitto
i molti modi di essere al mondo
resistono al delirio
disperato di sapere

XXVIII

se nella pozza del silenzio
il mio amore fa la tana
i giorni prendono fretta
le lune nuotano in cieli di cartapesta
e vedo il mondo dietro un velo
di leggerissimo rammarico

poi il mio amore
non sa che farsene di questo mio sogno di poco conto
in un'alba necessitosa

XXVII

beauty is in itself a kind of love
settled in the gaze
the desert of memories
of kisses of caresses of breaths
reaching to the edge of the sky
headlong
there are many ways of being in the world
resist the mad desperation
to know

XXVIII

if my lover makes his lair
in a pool of silence
the days seem rushed
the moons swim in false skies
and I see the world behind a veil
of slight regret

later my lover
does not know what to do with my trivial dream
in the impoverished dawn

XXIX

il letto sfatto di una notte non dormita
il mio amore tra le dita
appiccicoso e amaro

XXX

il mio amore numero trenta
unico e trino nella luce del mattino
bianco e solenne come un tonfo
e il passero sul davanzale

noi cerchiamo vanamente
di non sbiadire

XXIX

the unmade bed of a night without sleep
my love between
the sticky and bitter fingers

XXX

number xxx my love
single and triune[7] in the light of morning
pale and solemn like a loud thud
and a sparrow on the windowsill

we seek in vain
not to fade away

---

[7] This phrase refers to the trinity in Catholicism. The speaker and his lover are the "father and son."
They are a bit like the same person, and in a certain respect this love also gives birth to the "holy
spirit." In a "perfect" love, something more is born, a third spiritual element (though in this case it is
strange, because it is a love made up of a single person and another, one and two).

XXXI

il mio amore ha una bugia a mezza voce
di chi sa che la solitudine non esiste
esistono corpi separati e negletti
nel covo della notte
tra le mani del giorno

XXXII

parla allora la tregua del giorno
la vita sporca di terra
il passato che non vuole passare
o peggio ancora la distanza
tra un corpo bianco e una voce di polvere

dimenticato in un angolo come uno straccio
il mio amore giace stupito
e non respira

XXXI

my love is a lie spoken in an undertone
my lover knows that solitude does not exist
that there are separate and neglected bodies
in the lair of night
between the hands of the dawn

XXXII

speak then the truce of the day
this dirty life in mud
the past that haunts us
or even worse the distance
between a pale body and a voice of dust

forgotten in a corner like a rag
my love is astonished
and can't breathe

XXXIII

la distanza sconsiderata tra te e te

XXXIV

gemello dell'eternità
il mio amore non s'incarna e non teme
l'usura corre
e dura
fino alla soglia dell'ultima soglia
fino al silenzio al rostro
di una pazienza atroce
si ripiega su se stesso
sull'assenza di voce e di senso
prende tempo
e non dipende dalle umane cose

XXXIII

the reckless distance between you and yourself

XXXIV

my lover the twin of eternity
un-incarnate so he doesn't fear
the wear and tear
and will last
up to the threshold of the final threshold
up to the silence of the eagle's beak
of an unspeakable perseverance
my love is inward-looking
silent and beyond words
it is slow
and it does not depend on human things

XXXV

"e pensavo dissi
che noi quasi piangendo dissi
e volevo dire
e quasi mi soffocava davvero il pianto
che noi"

XXXVI

"non è vero che le parole"
volevo dirti questo
amore!

ma anche la vita non basta
a se stessa
è tessuta vanamente
trattenuta quel poco
freme come il sasso
che rimbalza due volte e poi
scompare

XXXV[8]

"… and thinking (I said);
that we (I said, almost weeping);
(and I wanted to say,
but it almost stifled me, really, as I wept;
that we …"

XXXVI

"It is not true that the words …"[9]
I wanted to tell you this
my love!

but life in itself
is not enough either
it is vainly constructed
withholding all the facts
it trembles
as the stone
that bounces twice
on the surface of the water
and then disappears

[8] XXXV is an excerpt from Edoardo Sanguineti's poem, "Oh, dove." The poem continues: "I wanted to say: with a love like this, we): / one day (we); (and the band was in the square, and the room was / in a strange twilight); / (we) are going to die:" Lepori inserts "che noi," at the end of the excerpt above, altering Sanguineti's poem, and creating a certain ambiguity.

9 "it is not true that the words create facts." from Pierre Bourdieu's *Language and Symbolic Power*.

XXXVII

brevi bolle di voci
salgono e lente
da una memoria circospetta

alcune sono carnali e feroci
altre appena accennate
a malapena provate

eppure crescono come piante maligne
nel rovescio del verso
nutrendosi di scaglie di pelle
di seme fresco gettato alle ortiche
di fragili segnali di fumo
dentro uno sguardo qualunque
dentro sera
e una volta posate nel cerchio
inesatto della voce
restano intatte come fossero
reliquie di te e di noi
baci umili del mondo

XXXVII

brief bubbles of voices
rise slowly
from a cautious memory

some are carnal and fierce
the other just mentioned
was hardly tested

yet they grow like malicious plants
on the other side of the verse
feeding themselves on flakes of skin
on fresh sperm thrown away[10]
on fragile smoke signals
inside any gaze
in the night
and once you place them in the circle
of the inexact voice
they remain intact as if they were
relics of you and us
humble kisses from the world

---

[10] The thrown seed recalls Onan, who was accused of the sin of masturbation in the Bible (Genesis, 38), or the sodomites (who do not fertilize).

XXXVIII

il mio amore ha la pelle dura
nella luce gialla della città sotto la pioggia
il mio amore finge indifferenza e incrocia le gambe
non sa neppure che lo sto guardando
e guardandolo lo creo
con la minuscola piega
quasi un taglio
sopra l'occhio
e la frangia di traverso

poi d'improvviso le parole mancano
e il suo viso si evapora
le mani sfuggono
orfeo

XXXVIII

my lover is tough
in the yellow city light in the rain
my lover fakes indifference and crosses his legs
he doesn't even know that I'm watching him
and looking at him I recreate him
with a tiny crease
almost a cut
above the eye
and the side-swept bangs

then suddenly the words are missing
and his face evaporates
the hands slip away
orpheus

XXXIX

gocce d'inchiostro in una pozza gelata
svelti disegni d'acqua su una pietra rovente
o nel greto del fiume e della notte
volti a milioni proiettati sullo scorrere

non ha bisogno di un nome
il mio amore
ma non per questo è un amore generico
basta una frase provvisoria
a ridargli densità

ma sempre più spesso
manca

XXXIX

drops of ink in a puddle of water
quick sketches with water on red-hot stone
or on the stones of the stream and during the night
you turn to millions of faces projected onto the water

without need of a name
my love
is not a generic love
just a provisional sentence
to give him density

but it's frequently
missing

XL

la litania di questa voce
amore!
svuotata dal di dentro e disponibile
quaranta piccole canzoni
vincono la paura
e durano fin dove
dura il fiato

XLI

poco oltre c'è il vento
la pula le chiacchiere
ma da chi vengano e chi parla
a chi si rivolgano e che dicono
sono domande inutili
inutilmente prostrate

quanto manca
alla fine della notte?

XL

O love!
the prayer of this voice
emptied from the inside and available
forty little songs
that defeat fear
and last until
the breath ends

XLI

it's windy over there
the losers make small talk
but who goes there and who speaks
and to whom do they turn and speak
useless questions

what of the night?[11]

---

[11] The phrase is from Isaiah (21: 11): "Watchman, what of the night."

XLII

vorrei piegare il capo
sul tuo braccio
e aspetto l'ora del cane
del lupo
per morderti sul collo
e inventarti i lineamenti
amore!
di un amore
preso a prestito dal sonno

XLIII

con un vantaggio evidente:
l'ombra gracile della volgarità
l'anatema dei giorni dispari
non può sfiorarlo
sfigurarlo
il mio amore è perfezione
e se occorre rinunciare alla tangibile
presenza di un nome
rinuncerò

(zoppo e ridicolo)

XLII

I would like to fold your head over your arm
and wait for the time of the dog
of the wolf
to bite your neck
and to reinvent your features
O love!
features of a love
borrowed from sleep

XLIII

with an obvious advantage:
the delicate shade of vulgarity
the anathema of odd days[12]
cannot touch him
or disfigure him
my lover is perfect
and if it's necessary to renounce
the tangible presence of a name
I renounce it

(imperfect and ridiculous)

---

[12] This refers to the *Cantata for Odd-Numbered Days* of Eduardo De Filippo, a series of texts dealing with common misery caused by the difficulty of life after the war.

XLIV

non ho che questa vita
per questo la raccolgo
nella rete di parole
cieche come mosche
e poi le vesto e le rivesto fino all'alba

l'attesa la presenza la tua presenza
sono fragili fiati del mattino
ma rifiuto il sospiro e la tempesta
perché conosco l'amarti più vero
quello che tocca pelle e che dispiega
un canto concavo

quello che gente onesta chiama speranza
ed io luce degli occhi

XLIV

I have nothing but this life
and this is why I created him
from the network of words
blind as flies
and then I dress and redress him until dawn

his presence awaits your presence
these fragile whispers in the morning
but I resist the sigh and the fury
because I know what is most true about love
is the touching of the skin and the unfolding
of a conciliatory song

what honest people call hope
and what lights up my eyes

XLV

mi chiedi un piccolo sforzo
un ultimo sforzo

ma senza motivo e senza schianto
qualcosa si spegne come si era acceso
sulla valle che diventa nebbia
qualcosa chiede che la voce si faccia sibilo
e si allontani nel bianco com'era venuto

non me ne devi volere
né piangere
questa lampada lasciata sulla soglia per troppo tempo
ha accettato che il vento
le desse il buio

e allora ti lascio andare
mio amore disperatamente immaginato
non ho diritti sul tuo cuore
né ferite né battaglie
il gesto quieto di una mano
il canto lontano

ti lascio andare
quasi amore

XLV

you're asking me to try harder
a final effort

but without reason and without violence
there is something that extinguishes him and just then
the valley becomes misty
something asks that the voice finish hissing
and return to the blank from which it came

do not be angry with me
I don't want to cry anymore
this lamp left on the threshold for too long
accepted the wind
that quenched its flame

and so I let him go
my desperately imagined lover
I have no rights over your heart
neither the wounds or the battles
the calm gesture of a hand
the faraway song

I let you go
quasi-love

NOTA

(*facoltativa*)

Che il mistero dell'amore debba riassumersi nella polarità tra un godimento fisico illimitato e una vaporosa perdizione romantica, mi sembra una grande sciocchezza. Vi sono forme d'amore – sia fisico sia spirituale – che sfuggono agli accadimenti di quella che per convenzione chiamiamo realtà. Di reale, dice Jean-Luc Lagarce, esiste solo il dolore fisico e la morte. Con questo poemetto ritrovo lo stupore giovanile per i lirici greci, per Penna e Saffo, e una voluta ingenuità. Racconto un'avventura emotiva che probabilmente è molto più diffusa di quanto le convenzioni sociali vogliano farci credere. Si può nascere alla vita in molti modi: pianta, sasso, torrente o personaggio, dice Pirandello. E le forme d'amore non si limitano ai fatti e alle cronache. Sono, avantutto, letteratura. « *Une des façons de parler d'un poème est de dire qu'il est un chemin, c'est-à- dire une expérience, une construction lente d'un rapport à soi, au monde, à la pensée, avec l'idée que la littérature (il n'y a pas d'exclusive du poème) est une façon de produire des formes de vie.* » (Stéphane Bouquet)

A BA, LC e JS

NOTE

That the mystery of love should be summed up in the polarity between unlimited physical enjoyment and a vaporous romantic perdition seems to me great nonsense. There are forms of love – both physical and spiritual – that escape the events of what we call reality by convention. What is real, says Jean-Luc Lagarce, is only physical pain and death. With this sequence of poems, I rediscover my youthful amazement for the Greek lyricists, for Sappho, and for Sandro Penna, as well as a desired naïveté. I tell an emotional adventure that is probably much more widespread than social conventions want us to believe. It can be born to life in many ways: plant, rock, stream or person, says Pirandello. And the forms of love are not limited to facts and chronicles. They are, above all, literary. "*One of the ways of speaking about a poem is to say that it is a path, that is, an experience, a slow construction of a relation to oneself, to the world, to thought, with the idea that literature (there is no exclusive poem) is a way of producing life forms.*" (Stéphane Bouquet)

About the Author

Pierre Lepori was born in Lugano (Switzerland) in 1968; he obtained a doctorate in drama from the University of Bern and trained in directing at the Lausanne High School of the Arts. Translator and poet (2003 Schiller Prize for *Qualunque sia il nome* (Whatever the Name)), he has published four novels (*Grisù, Sessualità* (Sexuality), *Come cani* (Like Dogs), *Effetto note* (Night Scenes)) which he himself translated into French. He founded and directed the queer magazine "Hétérographe" (2008-13) and is a translator of poetry and drama (Laederach, Roud, Pirandello, Penna ...). For the theatre, he created *Sans peau* (Without the Skin) (Théâtre 2.21), *Les Zoocrates* by Thierry Besançon (Lausanne Opera, with François Renou), Klaus Nomi Projekt and Le *Voyageur insomniaque* (The Sleepless Traveller) (Sandro Penna).

About the Translator

Peter Valente is a writer, translator, and author of twelve books, including a translation of Nanni Balestrini's *Blackout* (Commune Editions, 2017), which received a starred review in *Publisher's Weekly*. His most recent book is *Essays on the Peripheries* (Punctum books, 2021). Forthcoming is his translation of Gérard de Nerval, *The Illuminated* (Wakefield Press, 2022) and his translation of *Nicolas Pages* by Guillaume Dustan (Semiotext(e), 2023). Peter makes his home in Castle Hayne, North Carolina.

Printed in January 2022
by Gauvin Press,
Gatineau, Québec